Because She's A Lady

Copyright © Faye Jones Howard, 2013
Published by ZION Promotions LLC
PO Box 285, Winterville NC 28590
Email: fayec46@aol.com
Website: www.fayehoward.com

Cover Design: Alegna Media Suite
www.alegnamediasuite.com
Printing: Createspace
Interior Design: Humanitree House
www.humanitreehouse.com

Because She's a Lady
Howard, Faye
ISBN-13: 978-0615855769

Given To:

To Lady: _____

From: _____

Message: _____

_____

_____

_____

_____

_____

_____

_____

Thank You

A very special thank you to the women's ministry at the Philippi Church of Christ for your encouragement and trust.

Table of Contents

Chapter 1……..A Woman's Journey to Salvation

Chapter 2……………..…………..Creation Sings

Chapter 3…………………………………..In Service

Chapter 4………………..Lyrical Expressions

A Charge to Women

Dare you not step out, woman of valor?

Mother, wife, homemaker, counselor, compassionate listener, vision seeker, hope finder,

Friend, companion, defender of the brethren, Angel of mercy, pillar of grace, trusted of God, moving spirit, dare you not step out?

Dare you not step out? Did the Lord not choose you to be a woman of authority, the carrier of the seed?

Let us arise and go forth, for we are armed with the Strength of the Almighty.

Faith in God and what He can do is our sound foundation as we proclaim to the world,

"Is not the Lord gone out before thee"?

CHAPTER 1

A Woman's Journey to Salvation

Worship

As women, we express ourselves in many ways. We ask God for daily guidance, and we pray to Him for the smallest of things. In return, we are blessed with an abundance of compassion, thoughtfulness, power and strength.

Worship….

Total submission to the God

We cannot see…But we see Him.

To the God

We cannot touch…But we touch Him.

We worship Him In spirit and in truth;

For He is God

And God alone.

The Master Designer

Father, thank You for giving us the grace and
wisdom to wear the many hats that we, as women
of God, wear. You are the master designer, the
one who teaches us how to wear them.   When the
roles we play become overwhelming, You bid us to
lay our hats down at your feet. Your word comforts
and consoles us with the assurance that joy will
surely come in the morning. We rest with a new
strength and purpose, and we wake to find one
more beautiful raiment from Your creative hand.
Yes, another hat perhaps……….

Prayer of Dedication

& Affirmation

Master, today I will step into my identity.

I realize that I am highly favored.

I am the hope of generations.

I am the generation of hopes.

You have chosen me to sustain life,

To nourish, mold, and shape Your precious seeds.

You have bathed me in compassion, and

Listened as I cried out in the midnight hour,

Cried out for Your sons and daughters.

You have given me joy in the morning and

New mercies to carry me through the days.

I am a woman who is highly favored of God.

As I continue to walk in your light, I will not forget

my sisters, whom through circumstances, have forgotten who they are.

Eve has shown us that we can rise above our transgressions.

Hannah and Mary taught us to become handmaidens of the Lord, humbly depending on and receiving our strength from Him.

Peace

I am troubled today, Lord. Once again I seek Your comfort. Your word is steady and true. Today, I need to visit Your halls of consolation. I need to walk down Your corridors of truth and goodness. I anticipate the security that is soon to cover me like a warm blanket. I feel it as I go to Your word. I open the door. The words hit me. "Do not fret because of evildoers. Rest in the Lord and wait patiently for Him. Do not fret because of the man who brings wicked schemes to pass. Cease from anger and forsake wrath. Do not fret. It only causes harm." Thank You for the precious gift of peace. I am on solid ground once more.

I'm led to that place

Where the cool waters flow,

And peace like a river attends to my soul.

Through many a dark night,

I've surely been tried.

But His grace is sufficient,

And I am so satisfied!

The Mask

Take that mask off, sister!
Come on! Let's be real!
Scrap those nails and take off that mascara.
Get ready to shed some tears.
We seek a closer walk with God.
And yes, we have been deceived.
We have covered our hurts and pains
With new clothes and material gains.
Today, we seek a closer walk with God.
He knows us for the little girls we truly are.
He knows every heartache and pain
That has left us scarred.
Let our kindred spirits join in unison,
and let our knowledge
Of God and of each other be the healing force
That breaks up the rocky road we trod,
And brings us closer to one another.
This will enable us to have a closer walk with God!

A Prayer for Dieters

Oh Lord, help me to take care of my body and to remember that this is Your temple. I have to tear this temple down and restore it. It will take more than three days, but when I think of Your sacrifice, I realize how deep Your love for me is, and I strengthen for the task ahead.

You died alone, but I have You with me always to fight daily battles, no matter how large or small.

Today I shall embark on a restoration journey. Give me the strength to change my lifestyle so that I might better serve You.

Come on and eat the bread of heaven. Give God a living sacrifice. If you thirst, come to the river and fill your vessel with new life!

Butterfly

No one can still this ache

Within my soul but I.

Sometimes I can almost touch it

But like the butterfly

Who stops to taste the sweet nectar,

Knowing sweetness there abides,

Hesitates….and waits...

Then flies on by…

We all could be like this butterfly in one way or another. Why does the butterfly fly away? Perhaps it is afraid. We might not get it right the first time, but God provides the flowers, and when we are ready to take in the sweetness of His word, the nectar will still be sweet.

Sunrise

I remember my mother getting up early every morning. She would make her way to her favorite spot by the kitchen window where she would pray. It did not matter what was going on in the household, she thanked and praised God for everything! I did not understand it then, but through the circumstances of life, I have found myself walking in her footsteps.   I wait for Him in the morning, and I can hardly contain the majesty of the moment. I am a thirsty earth waiting for the morning dew.

As the thirsty earth awaits the morning dew;
I wait for you, to come and cover me;
Your mercies make me new.
I wait for you.
Your faithfulness is proven;
My direction comes from you.
Your loving light will lead me
To the things I need to do.
So I wait…
I wait for you.

The Window

I swear I was sitting at this same window 10, 20 or maybe even 30 years ago with the same problem on my mind; "how am I going to make it financially?" Maybe it was not this particular window, but it was some window, some dark and lonely room filled with depression.

What more can I do? How much more can I give of myself? I have lived my life for so many others, and all I want is a little peace for me. What did I do wrong? Lord, I offered You my life to do with as You pleased. Why is there so much struggle and suffering for me? I don't know what to do.

Should I listen to that still, small voice in my head saying, "give it up"? Should I just step out on faith? Should I listen to a friend of mine who is 450 miles away and to whom I haven't been in touch with for a while? Should I listen when she calls me in the middle of the night and tells me that she couldn't get me off her mind, and she had to call and tell me about trusting God and stepping out on faith? Should I listen?

I swear I was sitting at this same window 10, 20 or maybe even 30 years ago with the same praise on my lips; " Thank You God, for making a way out of no way"! Lord, I had almost given up. How did I manage to forget about the tenderness of Your mercies? How could I forget about Your loving kindness? You gave everything for me. You gave Your very life, and You did it gladly. It was Your pleasure. Every time I hearkened unto Your voice and every time I took that leap of faith, You were right where You said You would be, and You caught me. When I needed a word of confirmation, You sent me such a word that I knew it was You and only You. Then You spoke to my heart. In the midnight hour, the quiet of the night, You spoke to my heart, and I knew that You were with me.

As I sit at this window, I know that there are two presences with me. I can't lose because I know the one who prepares the window.

I find myself running back to Calvary.
That is where I find the peace I need.
There I lay my burdens down
Before the truest love that's found.
Yes, my comfort still rest in the cross.
Oh, my comfort still rest in the cross.

The Visit

Hello Lord. Here You are again, unexpected as always. If I knew You were going to "pop" in, I would have prepared a special place for You. I am in the middle of something, but as always, You know I will drop everything. These unannounced visits have become dear to me. I don't have time to get my Bible, but I feel myself entering the book as if I were entering a beautiful, familiar garden.

The fragrance of spirit and truth greet me at the entrance. Praise is in order. Time stands still. Tears of unspeakable joy fill my being. You are so near to me now. I can almost touch You and I am so amazed. My mind is clear, and I understand things that were complicated before Your visit. Discernment gives up its secrets and embraces revelation.

I see You, Lord, and it is wonderful! You did say that You would come before I called You!

Sassy Woman!

I use to live in the world
And then I got saved.
I didn't know I was on a journey
And the world was not about to behave
Just because I found some salvation.
The first thing the world sent to me
Was the man of my dreams;
Tall, dark and handsome
With a bag full of schemes
Designed to take my mind
And put me in a place
That only he could find.
But like I said,
"I use to live in the world."
This is what I told that fine brother…
"A book cannot contain me
Because God made me
And no man can write my destiny
Nor dissect my personality.
Just when you think you know me,
I'll be where you will never find me.
Good-bye!"

Lord of the Weights

Lord, sometimes life gets so hard;

It seems like I'm carrying weights.

Then I realize that You are Lord

Over all things.

You are also Lord over the weights.

Thank You

Lord, I thank You for the Holy Spirit that rescues me.

Thank You for the Holy Spirit that revives me. Thank You for the Holy Spirit that releases me. Thank You for the Holy Spirit that sets me free. Thank You for the Holy Spirit that does these things for me over and over again.

When my sun goes down, and they lay me to rest, I pray that I have done my best to live a life worthy of my Savior's sacrifice; to lift up His name through my life.

Love Expressed on Paper

I hesitate as I think about my feelings on love. I have this need to express my love on paper. My thoughts have constantly lingered on precious moments spent with family and friends, and my heart is filled with an indescribable fullness.

Sadness, joy, hopes and dreams, regrets, expectations, doubts and disappointments. These emotions flood my whole being and I cannot separate one from the other. They are all melded together and to take away one would create a void in my soul.

Without sadness, my joy would lose its flavor. Without regrets, my expectations, hopes and dreams would give little satisfaction, once accomplished. Disappointments can never be fully appreciated unless a victory can stand by its side.

I have come to learn that the spice of life is indeed bitter- sweet!

Has Your Love Got You Down?

There are people born with the capacity to love beyond love. They sometimes get lost in a maze of despair, hopelessness and depression. It is hard for them to function in what seems to be a "cold, cold world". Their hearts go out to the helpless, the homeless, the abused, the crippled, the hungry, and the unlovable. They carry the hurts of the lost. They feel their pain.

Are you one of these people? Has your love got you down? Don't you know that this kind of love is meant to lift you up? This kind of love is your armor and your weapon! It should be an honor to bear this kind of love. God has pierced your heart with the finger of compassion.

It's alright to cry in the night. Sometimes it may seem that your heart will break in pieces. It will not! Go to bed and take your rest. Wake to see the dawn of a brand new day and get to work. Work your ministry of love! You can make a difference!

You were born to!

Love has a color...

A color with no name.

It's the color of heartache.

It's the color of pain.

It's the color of sunshine.

It's the color of rain.

It's the color of my tears

Dried upon my face.

The Mother of Forgiveness

I am the mother of Forgiveness. Forgiveness is the product of all that I have learned in this life. I gave birth to her in much pain, agony and regret of unfulfilled dreams and aspirations. Forgiveness has been my open door giving me permission to "step out on faith" over and over again. She is the child of my heart and spirit. I realize now that she has always been with me. God gave her to me and in her innocence; I have found my place in the heart of the Master.

I cannot help but love her because she loves me unconditionally. This strange child is always full of hope. One would think that I taught her, but in truth, she has been my teacher. The child of my pain has become the child of my healing. The child of my suffering has become the child of my rejoicing.

Forgiveness has always been extremely demanding and needing so much from me. Those needs taught me patience. She saw life through a child's eyes and being her mother, I had to see things through her innocence and purity. She has led me to compassion, love, hope, longsuffering, gentleness and humbleness. If I had not given birth to this beautiful creation of God, I would be lost, not only to myself and family, but to my Savior.

I was not the first to birth Forgiveness. She was the gift from the cross. Did Jesus not say, "Father, forgive them"? Then I was given this gift to be birthed in my time of need.

I am the mother of Forgiveness.

Evening Prayer

Fill me with your compassion, Lord; Compassion that knows no limit. Clean me through and through. Give me new love, new hope. Make me over. Reconstruct this beaten vessel and reshape me, mold and make me usable and pliable enough to serve you one more day.

Morning Prayer

The beauty of your sunrise clouds my memory of the trials of yesterday. All that matters at this moment is this brand new day. Once more, your Son has truly risen in my heart, and I thank you.

Chapter 2

Creation Sings!

A Minute's Dream

Oh, the places one can visit in a dream! It only takes a minute, and the mind can weave a fantasy of unbelievable proportions; transforming one from a teenager who was on her way to the "out house", to a beholder of life, the seen and unseen wonders of this earth. A writer is born; a poet, an appreciator of creation and of the Creator.

A Minute's Dream

The world in all its splendor

Has made my heart surrender

To the beauty of the days

And all of God's mysterious ways

The grass beneath my feet so green

It seems as if in a dream

I beheld a sky of blue

With snow white clouds of summers' brew

A distant mountain covered with snow

Trees in autumn with leaves all aglow

A spider's web like lace is spun

Dew on a flower kissed by the sun

A morning glory so shy of the days

And seldom taste the sun's golden rays

But enfolds itself as curtains drawn

And in the early hours, welcomes the dawn

The mighty waves of a restless sea

Forever roaming, forever free

Seagulls fluttering everywhere

Without a worry, without a care

The awe and mystery of it all

The sun that shines, the rain that falls

The air I breathe, this world so free

These are the things God gave to me

The many wonders of this world

A sparkling diamond, a mother of pearl

The mystery of the things unseen

The glory of a minute's dream

Majestic Glory

Sunrise kisses the morning dew.

Birds sing and life is born anew.

A gentle breeze whispers to the trees;

My heart begins to sing.

Majestic glory!

His love surrounds the earth.

Majestic glory!

Throughout the universe

His name is written;

And it is plain to see

His majestic glory in me!

He Willed It So

How can a flower bloom in winter?

Live in cold and snow;

Face the elements with fragrance sweet?

I think I've come to know…

The Savior willed it so.

The radiance of the sun and moon

Sings a silent melody,

While creatures of the earth below

Proclaim His majesty!

All is Well

Today I will commune with the maker of the sea.

I will walk with Him on distant shores and feel the

sand beneath my feet. All is well…all is well.

He Delights in Me!

Listen; hear the sound of a distant thunder
Feel the earth tremble and see the hills shake
He comes!

Smoke flowing from His nostrils and fire from His
mouth
Consuming everything in His path
The one who set the world on its foundation
The one who gives breath to the wind
And warmth to the sun

The one who gives fragrance to the flower
And sweetness to the honeycomb
Through the darkness of clouds and storms, hail
And lighting, He comes
Terrible and tender

He comes!
Because I called Him!
He delights in me, and He will move heaven and
earth
In order to show me His perfect way!

Seasons

Through the seasons of my life, You stand, solid as a rock.

You are my building block,

Guiding me through winter storms;

Becoming my spring revival when things go wrong.

In summer, You are my refreshing breeze.

Through the fall of my changes, You never cease to meet my needs.

Thank you for my seasons!

The Seed

I must do as the spirit leads me.

I can feel His presence near.

My heart, my hands, my head respond in unison as His will becomes so clear.

He claims the seed within me.

It struggles to be free, to live in the paradise promised in eternity.

One day my earth will be fertile.

The seed will break through the sod.

Like leaves my arms will open wide, as I go to meet my God.

He is the planter of my hopes and dreams.

He is the one who made them grow. He is my Great Provider, my everything.

Oh, how I love Him So!

The Future

I AM the promise made before the foundation of the world.

I AM the song that fell from the lips of the prophets of old.

I AM an empty canvas; the unwritten story.

I AM the keeper of dreams.

I AM the future; the holder of destinies.

I AM the fingerprint of the Almighty.

I AM the future, laid out for God's good pleasure.

So, prepare the way of the Lord.

My glory shall cover the earth.

Surely, I come in the power and in the strength of He who has spoken it.

So shall it be!

Chapter 3

In Service

Just As You Served

As I kneel at Your altar, Lord,

I offer my body and my soul.

Please totally consume me;

Your fire will make me whole.

Burn Your words into my spirit;

Fill my heart with a new song.

I long to walk in Your footsteps

And lead others to the throne.

I want to live every day lost in Your word.

Lord, I want to serve just as You served.

I want to know Your compassion and undying love.

Lord, I want to serve just as You served.

As I enter into Your service, Lord,

I am available for Your use;

A living, breathing sacrifice,

With even greater works to do.

Give me wisdom from Your storehouse,

To minister tender grace;

To give hope to the hopeless ones

And show men a God who saves

The Church

I have stood through the ages.

I have watched your babies grow into men and women nourished by your prayers.

I have gathered your broken dreams, and my foundation has housed your tears. I welcome your joys, your pains and your sorrows. I encourage your hopes and dreams. I am the church. I am the altar of assurance to all who will come.

I am your church. It is my pleasure to be a haven for the homeless; a fortress for the oppressed; a heart fixer for the hurt; company for the lonely; a doctor for the sick; food for the hungry; rest for the weary and a path for the lost.

I am your church. Sanctified, ruled and cared by Jesus, the Christ, who is the head. I am the heartbeat of God, the body of Christ. I am your church! So celebrate, rejoice, for it is settled in heaven. We are the church! Alive and well!

We are the Church!

Servant of the Most High God

You are our servant;

The servant of the most high God.

By the life you lead,

Your good works and kind deeds…

We see His heart in your heart.

You are our servant.

You have been chosen to preach to a dying world;

In season, out of season,

Wherever it may be heard.

Preach the word!

Preach the word!

Preach the word!

The Old Soldier

Dedicated to Pastor Royal 2000

After the service had ended

With a closing prayer having been said

The old soldier looked upon the battleground

And the troops who he had led

With a look of tired triumph

He counted victories he had won

All for the love of Jesus, God's only begotten Son

His own wounds he did not notice

For his banner read "fight on!"

Then God said "bring him in for a little while

Repair work needs to be done"

Now he is back on the battleground

And he looks even better than new

There will always be an abundance of new recruits

And plenty of work to do!

Our First Lady

Dedicated to all First Ladies

You are a blessed woman!

You were chosen to be

The armor bearer for our servant!

Surely, faith has been your foundation.

Your quiet spirit radiates humbleness

And submissiveness, which comes

Only from God.

Thank you for your silent endurance…

For being a doer of the word…

And an example to all!

The Lady Preacher

She sat there in the pulpit

Quiet and humble as she could be

She had a message to deliver

It needed to be set free

She had to stay calm

And try to keep in line

She could have exploded

But this was not the time

The anointing was upon her

I could see it on her face

She struggled to control the gift

That would soon manifest in this place

Anticipation reached its peak

When through her glory cloud

She began to speak

Anointed words that hit the air

And began to change the atmosphere

Glory, glory filled this house

And stripped us of our earthly ware

Glory, glory filled this house

For the word Himself was here

He redressed us in heavenly clothes

And unspeakable joy filled our souls

Yokes were broken and deliverance proclaimed

To all who called on His holy name

Let us remember as days go by

Even though God is doing a new thing

In the earth and in our lives

This anointing is just the same

As it was when Jesus came!

The Mother of the Church

A walking song of life…

Her steps are precise;

Her ways are sure.

She is beauty, matured.

She can make you "check" yourself

With just a mere look!

Senior Citizens

Tried and retried…
Yet ever standing
Ever strong

You lift the hopes and aspirations of the new seed
with your wisdom of the past

You propel us into our future, daring us to be as
courageous and strong as you were

Tried and retried…
You embrace this world of change and encourage
us to follow a faith that has not changed like the
times

So we gladly take the baton and we shall pass it on
until the day we sit in the spectator's seat to cheer
others on

That is what we do…
We are senior citizens!

A Servant and a Friend

You have been with me all my life
And You have never changed.
I have seen your face in my mother's eyes
And tasted Your sweetness
In a summer's rain.
You laughed with me
Through my many joys;
You helped me to face my fears.
And when it seemed the pain
Would never stop;
You gently dried my tears.
I walk in Your footsteps
And though it gets hard;
Serving You is the greatest reward!

Daughters of Eve

Mother to Daughter

Daughter, I give reverence to you.

You are the extension of me;

My hope, my future,

My recovered dreams…

Through you, I live.

You are my heartbeat, my little girl;

My gift from God destined to be

A living song of life.

I celebrate you for the woman

You are and the woman you are

Destined by God to be.

Daughter to Mother

Mother, I give reverence to you.

My strong tower, my faith walker,

My builder of hope, my cleft in the

Rock, my lifesaver, my instructor;

My confidant and my best friend.

You are my living song of life.

Your prayers on my behalf have

Shaken the heavens!

I will wear your teachings

Daily in my heart!

I celebrate you for the woman you are.

Tribute to a Mother Gone Home

Don't you weep now.
Don't you cry!
Who else could care for her like the Lord?
Who owns her every tear drop?
Who holds her reward?
Don't you weep now.
Don't you cry!
She is in a place where you and I
Can only dream about.
This is not a fairy tale…
There is a higher plane.
She stepped into it without assistance
From a cane, a walker or any person.
Today, sickness bowed and pain ceased to be;
Today, the Holy of Holies, reigned supreme.
Humble yourselves…
Today we are all witnesses to a moment reserved
For each one of us.
Close your eyes and feel a free spirit as it
Meets its destiny and goes
From glory to glory to glory.
Don't you weep now!
Don't you cry!
Celebrate that life.
Now celebrate this life!
The life we can only dream about until that
Moment in time that is reserved for us alone.
To each, his own…
That special place of total grace.
Don't you weep now. Don't you cry!
Celebrate this life…

Perfect in Christ

He spoke to me through my heart

And suddenly, I knew;

The perfection that we seek,

Comes not from the words we speak;

But from the deeds we do!

Mary's Song

My heart doth sing;

My heart is free.

His works no longer hide in me;

For He has risen, for the world to see.

My child, my son;

He is now my King!

Building Bridges

Your spirit has stood through the ages.
Generations have been nourished by your prayers.
History records you, time and time again,
Making ways out of no ways;
Building bridges on dreams created out of blind
faith.
We reverence you, women of God, past and
present.
You are the bridge; the strong foundations
Holding up and supporting weaker beams.
This is our legacy.
We pass it on.
Always on the move…
Sometimes not appreciated, sometimes not
wanted,
Sometimes abused and misused;
But we keep moving,
Molding, shaping, lifting…
Building bridges…
Bridges of hope and forgiveness;
Bridges of survival and growth;
Bridges of love and encouragement;
Bridges of restoration and most of all,
Bridges of love.
We can do nothing without love.
We know that when we work together in love;
We bind ourselves to one another and to God,
Who is the Master Builder!

Building Bridges to the other Side

We are women on a journey.
We're building bridges to the other side.
God has given us a vision;
And a passion to serve mankind.
Chosen vessels, highly favored,
We have stood the test of time.
With unity and love abounding,
We're building bridges to the other side.

If Mary Could

I heard a voice so sweet and clear;

It spoke to me through my heart.

It said that I would carry the Word.

I said, "Lord, where would I start?

I am so young and who would believe,

A word from You, I could conceive?"

Then, I had a revelation.

There was a lesson and a plan.

If Mary could carry the Son of man

Surely, I can…

Carry His Word!

Chapter 4

Lyrical Expressions

Birth

Through rivers of heartache,

God sent me an island of peace

To rest and recover on.

He sent words and melodies

That comforted and consoled me;

And in the calmness of midnight,

My spirit gave birth to a song…..

Let the Blood Flow

Verse

The cross to me, use to be, a symbol of suffering and pain

I did not see that it could lead to a treasure of heavenly gain

In my search for Him, I began to trace the walk that took my place

As I understand, this is God's plan, in reverence, I say...

Chorus

Let the blood flow
Let it flow from Calvary
Let the blood flow
It transfigures you and me
Let the blood flow
It is our victory
Let the blood flow
From Calvary

Verse

God's only Son chose to come to the earth in the fullness of time

And live a life of sacrifice that His Father might be glorified

On His knees, in agony is where the choice was made

If this cup can't pass from me, Father, have your way and
Chorus

Up, Up and Away

Verse
They say there's a treasure just over the rainbow
With such beauty to behold
They say there's a river with love overflowing
And all the streets are paved with gold
My table is laid out; my mansion is waiting
I'm spreading my wings one day
When I hear the trumpet, I'm gonna be ready
I'm going up, up and away

Chorus
Up, up and away
Past the moon and the stars
Up, up an away
Past the Milky Way
I'll be that bright light
Shooting upward to glory
Don't cry, cause I'm going
Up, up and away

Verse
I hear joy bells in heaven ring out the glad tidings
As they lead me to His throne
What will it be like when the Rock of the Ages
Welcomes me to my new home?
I can't wait to dance with the heavenly angels
And to hear what the prophets say

When I tell them the story of my trip to glory
When I went up, up and away
Chorus

Heaven

Verse
There's a city that shines
All of the time
Its light never grows dim
There's a throne that sits high
Angels draw nigh
To forever worship Him

Chorus
Heaven is where the sun sets
And where it rises each morn
Heaven is the heartbeat of Jesus
Heaven is where we belong

Verse
There's a river that flows
Through streets of pure gold
In the midst stands the tree of life
I have this yearning inside
I long to reside
With my Savior in paradise

Chorus
Heaven is where the sun sets
And where it rises each morn
Heaven is the heartbeat of Jesus
Heaven is where we belong

Be it Unto Me

Verse
You have lifted me
You have exalted me
Generations shall call me blessed
I adore You, Lord
I magnify Your word
I worship Your holiness
With You, all things are possible
I reverence Your name
I surrender to Your will, my God
To the world I will proclaim

Chorus
Be it unto me, according to Your word
I humbly take my place, the handmaid of the Lord
(repeat)

Verse
This life inside of me
Is filled with destiny
To cry out in the wilderness
To adore You Lord
To magnify Your word
To worship Your holiness
With You all things are possible
I feel Him leap with joy
He knows that he is chosen
To prepare the way of the Lord

One Night with the King

Verse

They have made preparation
He is waiting for me
I enter His presence
With all I need
I present my gifts to Him
His praises I sing
I will change forever
After, one night with the King

Verse

He's the lover of my soul
I am favored, I am His
I go forth with gladness
For such a time as this
My heart feels the joy
The morning will bring
I will change forever
After, one night with the King

Bridge

When you give your life to Jesus, He will give you
everything
You will wear a crown of righteousness as one who
is redeemed.

Verse

The altar is open
He is waiting for you
To confess and believe that

His word is true
He's waiting with open arms
He has everything you need
You will change forever
After, one night with the King

Here you Stand

Verse

So here you are
The tears won't stop
Your hope is almost gone
With so much pain
A broken heart
Humbled, but not alone

Verse

So here you bend
Your tears all spent
Somehow you must go on
Covered with shame
Sick of sin
Humbled, but not alone

Verse

Now here you stand
A broken man
Before the Master's throne
Stripped of pride
But clean inside
Humbled, but not alone
Here you are, here you bend, and here you stand

.

Frozen in Praise

Verse
Let his moment last
I'm where I need to be
No reflections of my past
I can see eternity
I've been searching many days
To find this lovely place
Please let me stay
I want to stay here
Frozen in praise

Chorus
Cause I don't want to move
I don't want to think
I don't want to speak
I don't want to sing
All I want to do
Is stay right here with You
Frozen.........in praise
Frozen ....in praise
Second verse, Repeat 1st verse

I Pray for You

Verse
Your spirit is broken and your heart has grown cold
I have been chosen to carry your load
God has prepared me to run in this race
It is my pleasure to stand in your place

Chorus
I pray for you
I enter the session, where the saints of God gather
For holy direction, I lift you up high, I plead your
cause, I lay all your burdens before God's throne
I pray for you

Verse
My friend you may wonder how I know about you
I've been in the desert and someone prayed me
through
God gave us instruction; it's what He wants us to
do, He said to pray for one another as I pray for you

Chorus
I pray for you
I enter the session, where the saints of God gather
For holy direction, I lift you up high, I plead your
cause
I lay all your burdens before God's throne
I pray for you

Now I Know

Verse
I use to think that God was far away
I wasn't sure He really heard me when I prayed
But through the years, I have found He is the
source
And everything He created has a voice
Creation sings
So I will know

Chorus
I didn't know
You made me realize
You are the one
Who tells the sun when to rise
At your command
The seasons take flight
And you alone, know the secrets of the night
Creation sings
Now I know

Verse
Now I know
I have tasted your grace
I've felt your warmth in my mother's sweet embrace
I saw your smile on the face of my dad
The day he died, he left the greatest gift he had
He touched my heart, and now I know

Chorus

Now I can Love you Forever...

(A Wedding Renewal Song)

Verse
We once shared a life of heartache and strife
Who would believe we would be here today
To stand before God; to proclaim our love
And the beauty of His restoring grace

Chorus
Now I can love you forever
Christ made it possible
When all hope was gone
God said to hold on
I can love you forever

Verse
 God taught me to love and how to forgive
I thank you Lord for each trial in my life
For here stands the man I knew you could be
A man who has found the risen Christ

Verse
God taught me to cry, for He knew that I
Would find peace if I gave Him my tears
Now here stands my wife, the joy of my life
The woman whose faith bought back the lost years

Chorus

Tell It

Verse
Go tell the people, tell everyone
Wake up the sleeping, look to the sun
Tell the little children, tell men young and old
Tell the hurt and the lonely, tell every lost soul

Verse
Go tell the women weary from pain
Tell all the dreamers," you can dream again"
Go tell the prisoner, tell the jailer too
The worthless, the downcast, hope is here for you

Verse
Tell the poor in spirit, the kingdom is near
Tell all the mourners, the Comforter is here
Tell all who seek Him, great is their reward
The pure in heart and peaceful, the children of the
Lord

Bridge
Let all creation and every nation applaud His
majesty
Let all creation in celebration; sing out from sea to
sea
And tell it…
Go tell it.
Let's tell it! Tell it! Tell it! Let's tell it!
Our Savior is born!

Trusting and Believing

Chorus
Well I'm trusting and I'm believing
There are brighter days ahead
Oh yes I'm trusting and I'm believing
God will do just what He said
I may be in a barren desert
But He's my water; He's my bread
I keep on trusting, I keep believing
God will do just what He said

Verse
That old devil said to Jesus
If You bow down and worship me
I will give You all these kingdoms
I'll give You everything You see
Then Jesus told Him," be gone Satan"
Just get away from me
For it written, we'll worship our Lord
And serve Him only

Chorus
Because I'm trusting and I'm believing
There are brighter days ahead
Oh yes I'm trusting and I'm believing
God will do just what He said
I may be in a barren desert
But He's my water; He's my bread
I keep on trusting, I keep believing
God will do just what He said

Verse

So when the dark clouds gather round you
And you have no place to hide
When the winds of disappointment
Send troubles on either side
Just when it seems like you are sinking
Gods' strong hand will lift you high
Just keep on trusting, keep on believing
And lift your faith up to the sky

Chorus

Just keep on trusting
Keep on believing
There are brighter days ahead
Keep on trusting
Keep on believing
God will do just what He said
You may be in a barren desert
He's your water, He's your bread
Just keep on trusting
Keep on believing
God will do just what He said

Is this Gift for Me?

Verse
I stand in awe when I think about
The precious gift you gave to me
You dressed yourself in earthly flesh
And gave your love identity
I know I am unworthy of a love so divine
My mind cannot contain it
Is this gift really mine?

Verse
I stand in awe when I think about
That cold and barren place
Where I sought your forgiveness
Your mercy and your grace
I called out to a Holy God
Who reached out through time
And gave to me His only Son
Is this gift really mine?

Humble Beginnings

Verse
From humble beginnings
We've come thus far
Look where we started
Now look where we are
God's strong hand has bought us
We've fought for His cause
This church was established (Oh, yes it was)
By the blood of the cross

Verse
From humble beginnings
Came a church without walls
God's hedge of protection
Surrounded it all
And down through the years
Our small church has grown
On the prayers of the old saints
Who said, "Church, carry on."

Verse
Now as we look over
The path we have trod
Through good times and bad times
We've grown in the word of God
And our humble beginnings
Have been well worth the cost
For our church is a beacon (oh, yes it is)
It's a light to the lost

The Deep inside the Deep

Verse
When I think about the deep inside the deep
Of your love
I ask myself, who am I
That you could be so mindful of
That you would give your life
Then I lift my soul to give you praise
Thanks for my nights
Thanks for my days
Thanks for the manna sent from above
Thanks for the deep inside the deep of your love

Verse
When I think about the deep inside the deep
Of your love
I ask myself, who am I
That you could be so mindful of
That you would give your life
Then I lift my soul to give you praise
Thanks for my nights
Thanks for my days
Thanks for the manna sent from above
Thanks for the deep inside the deep of your love

Bridge
Love so deep that it covers me
Every drop of your blood made darkness flee
Love so deep that it has no end
Love so deep, it hides me from sin

You Surround Me

Verse
You surround me, Lord
You are the air I breathe
The sky above my head
The earth below my feet
I cannot hide from thee
Your love won't let me be
You surround me

Verse
You have touched my heart
You know my every pain
When I am torn apart
You send your healing rain
You make me whole again
With all the joy you bring
You surround me.

1st Verse…repeats
2nd Verse…repeats

I Will Be Like Him

Verse
The God of all the universe
The maker of the land and sea
Promised in His word that I
Could live eternally
For when I see Him face to face
I will be changed and every trace
Of mortality will be erased
And I will be like Him

Verse
I find it hard to understand
The glory of His majesty
He made the world with one command
Yet, He considered me
He made it possible that I
Could stand before Him glorified
This is the purpose for my life
And I will be like Him

Chorus
I will be like Him exalted, as they lead me to the throne
The angels will sing loud and clear
Father, Your child has come home
I will be like Him in beauty; I will be like Him in might
I can't wait to step into His forever light

Verse
Then I'll hear my Savior say
Well done child, now come this way
I'll walk with Him down streets of gold
As the mystery unfolds
I'll comprehend His love so deep
And why He died for you and me
Then His joy will be complete
And I will be like Him

I Want More

Verse
Oh, I prayed that You would fill be
When I promised You my all
Then You poured Your presence on me
Like a cooling waterfall
Now I'm basking in Your glory
Seems I just can't get enough
I want to spend my every moment
Drowning in Your love

Chorus
I want more and more and more and more and
more and more and more
You can wash me in Your cleansing rain
Anoint me with your joy
I want more and more
That's all I'm longing for
Holy Spirit, lift me high
And open heaven's door
Jesus, I want more

Verse
And when I ride this wave of gladness
To the New Jerusalem
I will wade in crystal waters
Till I make my way to Him
And when He's standing there to greet me
Won't the angels be amazed?
To see me changed before their eyes
Shining in His grace
Repeat Chorus

Sunday Morning Tears

**3rd Place Winner Babbie Mason Music Seminar
2001 Songwriting Contest**

Verse
Once again we enter
The house of the Lord
And once again we gather
To receive His holy word
We bring our joys and sorrows
We bring our hopes and fears
And there God sends His sweet release
In Sunday morning tears

Chorus
Sunday morning tears can be just what you need
They can ease your weary mind
And set your spirit free
They can change your cold and stony heart
And make your visions clear
God puts something special
In those Sunday morning tears

Verse
It is so fulfilling to greet your neighbors and your
friends
To fellowship together with the hope that lives
within
We find out from each other that we are not alone
And when we gather round the altar
We are at the Father's throne...the Father's throne

Verse
We can give it all to Jesus
Our Savior and our King
He has made our tears His treasure
For we are His redeemed
And as we glory in His presence
And the dew of peace descends
He showers us with sweet release
In Sunday morning tears

Chorus
Sunday morning tears
Can be just what you need
They can ease your weary mind
And set your spirit free
They can change your cold and stony heart
And make your visions clear
God puts something special
In those Sunday morning tears

Jubilee!

2nd Place Winner Babbie Mason
Music Seminar 2002

Verse
We have trampled through the valley
We have sailed the stormy sea
We have found ourselves in bondage
We have seen ourselves set free
Now we gather on the mountain
To proclaim our liberty
As we praise our God who brought us
Church, it's time for Jubilee!

Chorus
Jubilee, jubilee, church it's time for jubilee
It's our dear Lord's year of favor
Church, it's time for jubilee

Verse
We have lived on crumbs of sorrow
We have caught the threads of hope
We have come up out of darkness
God has loosed old Satan's hold
Now it's time we rest from toiling
And rely on God's increase
While we trust Him for provision
Church, it time for jubilee

Chorus

Jubilee, jubilee, church it's time for jubilee
It's our dear Lord's year of favor
Church, it's time for jubilee
Jubilee, jubilee, church it's time for jubilee
It's our dear Lord's' year of favor
Church, it's time for jubilee
Repeat chorus

Because She's a Lady

From out of the ashes, steps beauty refined
How could she overcome the pain and still shine?
The enemy thought he had won the race
When this battered woman fell on her face
He didn't know that this was her position to pray
And because she's a lady, she decided to stay

Because she's a lady
She bows to authority
The fear of the Lord is her shield
She will move when He says to
She will do what He says do
She won't let go of His Will

Our heart's desire is to discover the purpose of God for our individual lives. No matter how misdirected or sometimes out of focus we may be; there is a deep truth hiding in our secret places where we keep our dreams and our wonderful things.
 God knows who we really are, and He comes to our rescue day in and day out. He knows our hearts because He made our hearts. He repairs us. He comforts and consoles us. He mends us in the darkness of our midnight hours, and in the morning, He wakes us with a whisper not heard by mortal man, but is heard in the throne room of our hearts:

**WAKE UP SWEET DAUGHTER...
YOU ARE STILL A LADY!**

The Author

FAYE JONES HOWARD discovered an appreciation for the worth of words at an early age. Her first published poem, "A Minute's Dream" was written when she was a high school senior. She placed second and third place consecutively in 2001 and 2002 in the Babbie Mason Music Seminar, which was her first songwriting experience. Faye is a member of the Nashville Songwriters Association International; Contemporary Christian Music Network International; and ASCAP.

Faye began making contributions to her church and community theater by writing materials for special events, including plays, church documentaries and women's conferences.

"Because She's a Lady" was born out of the women's conference writings that Faye contributed to the women's ministry at her church. It also contains other writings in reference to the church as a whole. This book honors the inspiration that came about as part of her experience with the women's ministry. Faye is sixty six years old and the proud mother of two children and grandmother of eight. She is working on her next book; *"Compassion… Like We Never Knew"*. She was diagnosed with stage four lung cancer in 2010. It is her hope that this upcoming book will minister to others with a terminal cancer diagnosis.

www.ingramcontent.com/pod-product-compliance
Lightning Source LLC
Chambersburg PA
CBHW062019040426
42447CB00010B/2074